FROM
Molested
TO *Majestic*

Valerie Harris

ISBN 978-1-63814-322-2 (Paperback)
ISBN 978-1-63814-323-9 (Digital)

Covenant Books, Inc.
11661 Hwy 707
Murrells Inlet, SC 29576
www.covenantbooks.com

I want to dedicate this book to those of you who have not quite understood the process of God in your life and also to those of you who are coming into your purpose. Sometimes it's hard to understand why you are holding a shovel in your hand when God promised you greatness! You never anticipated becoming all things until you had to become all things. Paul the Apostle said, "To the Jews I became a Jew that I may win some" (1 Cor. 9:20). Whatever God has created you for, you first must become it. If God is calling you to the brokenhearted, you become the brokenhearted!

Be encouraged, beloved! God himself is very crafty in his approach to bring you forward in all things. He is strategic in his ability to orchestrate every detail whether visible or invisible regarding your life. He, God, is a wise master builder that intends on bringing the best out of you that you may prove to be signed, sealed, and delivered. Quite often, there is a misconception of what God is doing in the life of the believer because it doesn't look parallel to the vision he gave you. Isn't it funny how God shows you the glory, but you didn't see the pit until you landed in it?

I dedicate this book to all of you that have hidden the Word of the Lord deeply in your hearts that you may carry out what is inside of you. I am so grateful to God for a great cloud of witnesses that encouraged me when I didn't think that I could come through the rubbles of life, but I did by the grace of God. There were times where certain messages from great men and women of God would minister to me deeply, and it gave me strength to push through no matter what. We all go through something, but be mindful how you go through because there is a crown that awaits you!

Contents

Introduction

All of us, no matter how successful, how poor, what religious background, or moral upbringing, go through a journey called life. Life distinguishes us from one another. It is the process of growth and development that shapes us into our future. Life yields unto us lessons that will forever change our trajectory and perception of how you respond to certain gestures whether they are good or bad. None of us gets to choose what family, environment, and culture we are born into, but we have the power to reverse the generational bondage that we inherit by renewing our minds according to the knowledge of Christ Jesus.

God will always process us to rid us of our prior and present baggage of abandonment, rejection, fear, resentment, unforgiveness, emptiness, rage, and self-consciousness. We all must walk through the steps of confession to receive deliverance in a way that His (God) truth becomes our truth. His truth is what makes us free. It is how He sees us and also what He has created us to be in Him. Acts 17:28 says, "For in Him we live and move and have our being."

In this book, I share some of my own personal experiences and what it took for me to move in a direction that was healthy and positive for my life. None of us are exempt from challenges, and it is those challenges that mold us into becoming stronger and better as long as we choose the right therapy. You will not always get it right the first time. We all deserve a second chance at being the best versions of ourselves, and God gives us a second chance!

The Beginning

I was born in Huntsville, Alabama, and I am the second child of three children born to my mother and father. My sisters and I grew up in absolute poverty. I remember walking to various places as a result of my parents not having transportation. My father seldom stayed employed due to his struggle with alcoholism. He was an authentic product of both his mother and father's generational irresponsibility. The accountability was not solely from him but the lineage he was derived. As, a result he made life unstable, unsecure, and unsure for us. After all, he was only a pattern of the generation before him.

Now, my mother always taught both my sisters and I to pray and to try to live a life that was pleasing unto the Lord. Consequently, we were taken from her parental custody and placed in a foster home on account of our quality of life at the time. My mother was into the process of divorcing my father in order for the courts to release us back in her custody, and this process took about a year and a half. While in the foster home, a seventeen-year-old foster minor took an inappropriate interest in me. He would come into my room late nights to wake me and then proceed to take me into the bathroom to have intercourse with me. I was only seven years of age, unprepared, unequipped, and unknowledgeable for what would come after this.

Finally, when my mother regained custody of her three children after divorcing my dad, I was so elated—believing that this phase of my life was finally over, but it was only the beginning. Painfully this sexual abuse somehow kept happening to me. No matter where I went, no matter where I lived, I found myself always being the victim of a repetitive cycle of sexual abuse. It then happened by a relative who was also a teenage boy of seventeen years of age, and it happened more than once as well as the first incident. At this time, I was eight and trapped again. I remember going to school depressed, wishing that someone could sympathize with my situation. I was afraid to mention this to anyone, though there were signs that something was happening, but no one was able to detect it or asked, "Is everything okay?" After both encounters with both teenage boys, there was blood in my underwear. Now when I was in foster care, my foster mother thought I was starting my menstrual cycle, and my biological mother, when in her care, took me to see a doctor, and he only prescribed cream. Years later, I thought that was oddly strange that a doctor who performed an examination could not discern something inappropriate was going on! This continued to happen throughout my life, but I have decided not to share the third abuser.

My Teenage Years

Truthfully, I was a very odd teenager! Even my friends were strange. I would choose to have conversation with individuals whom not everyone would commune with. I would find myself, in some way, wanting them to know that they were special and valuable. I was also very witty. I would be in my classes imitating ministers in my church and how they preached and prayed.

I truly enjoyed it, but it got me in trouble in the classroom setting, as I recall one of my teacher's saying to me, "Get out and go to the principal's office!"

As I started dating, keep in mind that I lost my virginity at seven years of age; I had mixed feeling about sex. On one hand, I thought that it was the most painful thing to engage in, but there was also a curiosity of what it really was like with someone special. When I turned eighteen, I was dating a young man whom I thought the world of at that time. He was very poetic like myself. We would have deep dialogues about life, marriage, and success. We would share poems with one another that we thought were profound masterpieces. Honestly, we lived in a fictitious world. We were dreamers with no real sense of reality, just imagination.

On the day of my eighteenth birthday, I told my mother not to wait up for me that night because I was going to spend the night with one of my friends. When realistically, I was going to celebrate my birthday with my poetic boyfriend. Prior to this day, for about three days, I debated whether or not I would have sex with him on my birthday. This debate was so strong in my spirit. I loved him but feared I would become pregnant. I said to myself, *With my luck, I will do it and get pregnant.*

My oldest sister already had her first child, and my youngest sister was pregnant with her first child, and I didn't think I was ready for that chapter of life. Unknowingly at the time, I didn't realize that this was God troubling my spirit because I was getting ready to embark upon a new chapter in my life. The chapter of salvation! Glory to God! I didn't do it!

Later some time, I saw my boyfriend's face on the news for killing someone. This case had not been solved for about a year because no witnesses would come forth. As you could imagine, I was horrified, dumbfounded, at a loss for words, confused, and shocked all at the same time. I was thinking, *Here is a young man whom I had talked about marriage with, and he has killed someone!* I instantly thought, *My boyfriend is a murderer.*

The day he was able to call me was an awkward and uneasy conversation. Even though he disclosed to me the details of what happened, I decided not to continue a relationship with him.

After such devastating news, I was in a very low place in my spirit. I felt as if my world had collapsed, and the person who was meant for me was no longer part of me. So, while coming from my oldest sister's apartment, one day, I told God that I was giving him my life because it had been filled with such pain, disappointment, and emptiness so often. I said that to God, not knowing that it was the time of salvation for me. God was using this situation as a vehicle to drive me into his presence at an appointed time. Not only that but also God was saving me from that life he never intended on me having with this young man, and as a result of that, God exposed what was going on in secret that I could not see to give me direction for where I was going in him. The next week, I found myself praying and reading the Word, and the profanity that always filled my mouth was no longer a part of my vocabulary. I began to wonder what was really happening with me!

The Process

As I was growing closer to the Lord, my mind was being attacked by the enemy.

The devil often reminded me, *If God love you so much, why did he let three persons sexually abuse you when you were a child?*

I want to take the time right here at this moment and teach you a fact regarding your adversary. It is important that you understand that the enemy will always try to destroy what God has placed inside of you. He wants to snatch your destiny. He doesn't wait until you are mature enough to handle it. He's an intruder.

Now, before I explain how God dealt with this reoccurring issue that was becoming magnified in my thoughts, let's look at the life of Joseph in the book of Genesis. He was the son of Israel. We discover that his beginning wasn't so glorious either. "But when his brothers saw that their father loved him more than all his brothers, they hated him and could not speak peaceably" (Gen. 37:4 NKJ). Understand that the enemy hates you because of what God has created you to do. If the devil cannot kill you, he will try to destroy you. And if he is unable to destroy you, he will try to steal your purpose in God.

When we examine Genesis 37:20–27, we see how the devil plotted to kill Joseph, but God prevented them from taking his life by allowing Rueben to speak up and delivered Joseph from his brother's hand:

> Come therefore, let us now kill him and cast him into some pit; and we shall say, "Some wild beast has devoured him. We shall see what will become of his dreams." But Rueben heard it, and he delivered him out of their hands, and

said, "Let us not kill him." And Rueben said to them, "Shed no blood, but cast him into this pit which is in the wilderness, and do not lay a hand on him"—that he might deliver him out of their hands, and bring him back to his father. So it came to pass, when Joseph had come to his brothers, that they stripped Joseph of his tunic, the tunic of many colors that was on him. Then they took him and cast him into a pit. And the pit was empty; there was no water in it. And they sat down to eat a meal. Then they lifted their eyes and looked and there was a company of Ishmaelites, bearing spices, balm, and myrrh, on their way to carry them down to Egypt. So Judah said to his brother, "What profit is there if we kill our brother and conceal his blood. Come and let us sell him to the Ishmaelites, and let not our hand be upon him, for he is our brother and our flesh." And his brothers listened.

People of God, can I tell you that no weapon formed against you shall not be able to prosper (Isa. 54:17). God doesn't get glory out of what is dead, dry, cripple, feeble, sick, broken, and lost, but he gets glory from quickening these things in our lives. There was no glory in my being molested by three different persons, but the glory was in God destroying the yokes of the matter by which happened by way of a generational curse in my ancestry. Satan tried his best to destroy my purpose in God by stealing my virginity and telling me God didn't love me when in fact, God delivered me from marrying a young man whom he had not chosen for me.

Understand that we can never go back and reset the past, but we can live in the present, predicting our future. God had given me power and knowledge over the will of the wicked one. Are you curious to know how God set me free from battling with sexual abuse? God is the only one who can bring revelation truth to you!

Remember when Jesus asked Peter, "Who do men say I am?"

Peter answered, "Some say John the Baptist, some Elijah, and or one of the prophets" (Matt. 16:13–14), and Jesus proceeded, "'But who do you say I am?' Simon Peter answered and said, 'You are the Christ, the son of the living God.' Jesus answered and said to him, 'Blessed are you, Simon Bar-Jonah, for flesh and blood has not revealed this to you, but your father who is in heaven'" (Matt. 16:14–17). So the revelation that God had given Peter superseded what Peter knew in the natural about Jesus! When God revealed this truth, his eyes became opened, and it changed his perception of who Jesus was. So, when God revealed to me by truth that this was a generational curse that I had undergone, it superseded my knowledge in the natural, thus opening my eyes to the deception of the enemy to place the blame on God when the devil himself was behind my heartache. Again, he was trying to steal my purpose in God.

Dismantling

Dismantling is something that all believers must go through because we have unknowingly and sometimes consciously placed a stony layer over our hearts to prevent futuristic hardships. Scripturally, the Bible teaches us to guard our hearts because out of it flows the issues of life (Prov. 4:23). But this doesn't mean we should be leery of showing emotions. My pain taught me how to mask my emotions by never wanting to feel such helplessness again. It taught me how to be abrasive. Pain alone should never be your teacher because pain will cause you to shut your heart from people including God, and that's not the will of God for your life. Pain must be accompanied by the Word of God. God uses pain, but the enemy does too. The devil has, from the beginning, tried to be like God, but he is a counterfeit. God is the authentic proof. Some of you may be wondering, *How is Satan a counterfeit when God made him an original?* Well the answer is a simple one. When we think of currency, especially dollar bills, if you have not been entrusted by the US Bureau of Engraving and Printing to print money, it is illegal to do so. If you do not reserve the rights to duplicate something, then you are an impostor. Lucifer was created for a specific purpose, but because he fell from that purpose and tried to lift himself above the throne of God, he became illegal. He did not reserve the rights to do so!

The devil uses pain to destroy, but God uses pain to break your will. I believe I'll say that again! God uses pain to break your will! In the dismantling process, you may feel as if you are losing pieces of yourself. Paul says it like this, "Yea doubtless, and I count all things but loss for the excellency of the knowledge of Christ Jesus my Lord: for whom I have suffered the loss of all things, and do count them but dung that I may win Christ" (Phil. 3:8). Oftentimes when we

15

are in pain, we look for healing or something to aid us. This gives God an open door to reveal himself to us. When the Word is present with pain, God can create a foundation to build on. We come to the realization that we are not perfect, and we need a savior and answers as to why we are going through what we go through. One will always lose what is unnecessary when they are in the perfect will of God to gain the knowledge of Christ. God breaks our will by uncovering his plan for our lives and giving us the fruits of the Spirit so that we are harmless as doves but wise as serpents (Matt. 10:16).

Psalm 34:18 teaches us that "the Lord is nigh unto them that are of a broken heart; and saveth such as be of a contrite spirit." You see, he will use anything to bring you closer in his presence. Every born-again believer must rid themselves of unbelief, unforgiveness, resentment, hate, anger, lust, covetousness, pride, selfishness, and self-righteousness. Before God dismantles you, he allows you to become stronger in your faith and your walk with him. He will answer prayers speedily and build you up with an intention to surgically go in and remove the residue and debris. For instance, he will allow a pastor or elder to rebuke you for your self-righteousness. This may hurt you in the beginning; however, the Spirit of God will begin to work on your heart to show you your unpolished self. Once your understanding is enlightened, you'll develop a desire to want to change and walk in his will as a result of him showing you his love toward you and his healing grace.

Development

J oseph went from being hated by his brethren, sold to the Ishmaelites into Pharaoh's house, lied on by Pharaoh's wife, and then into prison serving a sentence yet while he was innocent. Now, that's enough to force us all to say, "Lord, haven't I been through enough!" Your gifts are being cultivated while you are under pressure because the pressure is pushing what is lying dormant up and out. When I think of planting seeds, I always think how the ground must first be dug up in order for the seed to be planted or imparted. While the seed remains underground, no one can see it or suspects it there. Once it breaks out of its seed form, it grows underground first, forming roots. It then buds above ground where it is physically visible. Strangely, one would think, once the ground becomes muddy that nothing could possibly come up from the ground.

First Corinthians 15:36 says, "Foolish one, what you sow is not made alive unless it dies." Your gift will not become alive until it is buried, but the good news is the ground is filled with soil nutrients that will cause your crop to spring up. I know I just lost a few people there, but you don't truly know what's in you until it is forced to come up and out! There were incidents that I can remember that was in my life that were lifeless. Situations have stared me in the face where I've had to believe God by myself by faith in my pile of mess. Listen. There are things that God himself have handpicked and designed to develop your gifting.

If you are captivated by what is in this book, it is because it is a clear indication that you are pregnant with purpose, and God intends on you giving birth to something that's bigger than you! Now is not the time to give up. Your development in this process is vitally important to where you are going. Why does the seed have to die?

When we think of life, we think of living. When we think of death, we think of dying, but this passage of scripture above is the opposite. Let's consider the winter season as an example. We commonly observe leaves, flowers, trees, plants, and crops dying. The reason this is taking place is because winter is a harsh season. Without the proper necessities of the sun, heat, good soil, and water, none of these can survive, but trees will reduce themselves to their strongest part—their trunks. Plants will die in the winter and come up in the spring with such radiance because their root survived the toughest and deadliest season. The seed dies because it changes its bodily form. It breaks the shell it was originally in and is created or shaped into something that looks nothing like its beginning.

Can I prophesy to you? I want to tell you that God is allowing the old you to die so the new you can live and that your gift is being purged so that it can bring glory to the name of our God! God strategically gave Joseph wisdom, insight, and interpretation in prison. Sometimes God will allow you to be captive until the appointed time for you to come out. Remember how he tells Abraham that his descendants will be slaves for four hundred years, but he was going to deliver them (Gen. 15:13). God himself will walk us through humility. That will always be the key to keeping the anointing in your life. When you realize that you can do nothing on your own, but it takes the help of the Lord to deliver you and set you free, humility will become your best friend. Joseph had practiced on developing his gift before he was able to become a governor. He sat in prison for seventeen years, being taught by the hand of God before he was able to rule over. Waiting on God is not peaches and cream.

Waiting on God allows us to fulfill James 1:4: "But let patience have its perfect work, that you may be perfect and complete, lacking nothing." Waiting causes God's complete will to enter in our life. Quite often, we will suffer many things when waiting on the Lord. We will become frustrated, irritated, and even angry, but the waiting allows us to yield the fruit of the Spirit, which is love, peace, joy, kindness, longsuffering, goodness, faithfulness, gentleness, and self-control (Gal. 5:22).

Can you imagine being confined to a prison when you're actually innocent? Joseph is paying the price for a crime based on a false accusation that no one bothered to investigate. So, it is because it's Pharaoh's wife, who is bringing this charge against him, it becomes his punishment. Here is a man with a prophetic word from the God who came by way of a dream, and he has not yet seen the prophecy fulfilled. The prophetic word was a seed, and the seed was dying, buried in a prison so that the crop of his word could be formed. Don't tell me that God won't let you suffer many things in order for his Word to come to pass. I've been there before lamenting in my pain with no sense of direction, praying that God would pick me up out of this hellhole and allow me to have peace without the aftermath of warfare.

Let's call to remembrance the butler and the baker. They both were troubled in their spirit about a dream that they both dreamed individually (Gen. 40:9–14). When Joseph interpreted their dreams, the butler was thrilled. The baker was sad being that his punishment was death. Pharaoh had ordered his life to be taken in three days. God was allowing Joseph to develop and perfect his gift of interpretation. This is why all things work together for the good of them that love the Lord and are called according to his purpose (Rom. 8:28). When we are in the perfect will of God, our steps can be ordered by the Lord.

Deliverance

Deliverance is always an awesome victory because it brings freedom, but it also can be messy because of the process. We will, for now, focus on the victory portion. God divinely gave Pharaoh a dream that was alarming in his spirit. As a result of this, Pharaoh called for all astrologers, magicians, and wise men of Egypt to interpret his dream, but no one was able to do so. The butler remembered Joseph and told Pharaoh that there was a young Hebrew who was in prison who could interpret his dream. So, Pharaoh called for Joseph. Look at this. God was giving Pharaoh a dream that only Joseph's expertise could be used to provide understanding. At the right time, God had appointed for Joseph to be released and walk in his purpose and destiny.

Once Joseph had changed his attire and was shaved, he went in to see Pharaoh.

Pharaoh began to tell Joseph, "I understand that you can interpret dreams."

And Joseph responded, "It is not in me, but interpretation belongs to God."

Pharaoh began to tell Joseph his dream, and Joseph interpreted the dream. Joseph advised Pharaoh that he should set a wise man over the land to gather much and manage the economy, and Pharaoh appointed Joseph because of his wisdom and expertise in the things of God. God purposely had Joseph in the land that he would prosper in, but that word had to be tried. Joseph had to go through something in order to obtain the promise.

Sometimes God will allow you to endure hardship as a good soldier to bring your spirit into humility that once you are delivered, you won't forget the process or who brought you through the waters, the fire, the pain, and the struggle. You will be delivered into your promise with a "Yes, Lord, I will go, and I will obey."

My experience with deliverance has not always been a shouting experience. One in particular was a quiet deliverance. I hoped that someone would have helped me celebrate my glorious deliverance, but none was present to rejoice with me. I'm sure if Joseph's family had been present, he would have wanted them to host him a grand celebration, but he was alone, with none of his family's support. I have rejoiced inwardly for my deliverances being as no one else knew my story neither my trial. So I had to rejoice and encourage myself in the Lord. Too many times people look to others to bring out an orchestra or a massive band and cheerleaders releasing balloons, party graffiti, and shouts of praise only to find out that this is between you and God! There are private victories that God will prove to you that He is God! This will teach you how to totally yield your life to God so He can use you to the magnitude He intended you for. It's impossible to boast in your flesh when what God did for you could not be done so by the working of man. You will do like the apostle Paul and make your boast in the Lord (1 Cor. 1:31).

I want to pose a very important question: when God delivers you out of your trial, how does he deliver the trial out of you? It is one thing to be taken out of a mess, but how is the mess going to come out of you? Your mindset must change because you are still operating in trauma, confusion, brokenness, disappointment, and sometimes anger. Your mind has to be renewed with you. You now have to take on the identity of the Word that you may be washed thereby. Even though we make a decision to forgive people, it doesn't erase the fact that it still hurts because you are human. Sometimes the message of God can be preached or conveyed in such a way where it implies that we are superhuman, but the truth is we are emotional beings that feel and hurt. We must deal with the aftermath of our trial. Yes, we were brought out. Now I have to make sure it's completely out of me!

How do you know that you are free from issues of the past? Let's go back to the story of Joseph. When Joseph came face-to-face with his brothers, he broke down and began to cry. He truly missed his brothers, also had forgiven them, and gave them assurance that God, not them, had placed him where he was so that he could preserve life for them and their families (Gen. 45:1–8). The issues no longer have control over you. You yield a more peaceable fruit among those who have wronged you. I believe the hardest part of revisiting your past is having to face those who did you wrong, but if you have been truly set free, there's no bitterness. I can honestly say, of the three individuals I was molested by, I have seen two of them multiple times, and I actually felt sorry for them because they must get this thing right before God!

Disobedience

Disobedience is to resist or refuse the will of God for your life. I personally believe we engage in disobedience when our will is not completely broken. The perfect example of obedience is Jesus. Jesus is in the garden of Gethsemane praying and asking God to take something from him that seems too difficult to accomplish (Luke 22:42). Let's first establish that it is essential to have a prayer life because prayer will strengthen you to choose what is right like Jesus did. Without a consistent prayer life, you will begin to maneuver into a realm of flesh where you only obey what seems natural to do. I was always taught by my parents if someone hits you, then hit them back. But Jesus said if someone strikes you, turn the other cheek. It's not natural to not defend yourself. So, if God is saying to forgive someone who hurt you, you tend to hang on to unforgiveness as a form of justification for what you endured.

We must let the matters of yesteryears go, considering that we will not walk in our full potential of what it is that God is calling us to do. Also, we are wasting precious time by going around a mountain that we have the power to flatten and cause to become a plain by our obedience. I want to bring your attention to the prophet Jonah and his journey of disobedience: "Now the word of the Lord came unto Jonah the son of Amittai, saying, Arise, go to Nineveh, that great city, and cry against it; for their wickedness is come up before me. But Jonah rose up to flee unto Tarshish from the presence of the Lord, and went down to Joppa; and he found a ship going to Tarshish: so he paid the fare thereof, and went down into it, to go with them unto Tarshish from the presence of the Lord" (Jon. 1:1–3). Jonah had a clear message from God and what it was that God had assigned him to do, but he was refusing the will of God.

Now, let's go a step further and see what happens to Jonah as a result of his disobedience. Verse 4 says, "But the Lord sent out a great wind into the sea, and there was a mighty tempest in the sea, so that the ship was like to be broken" (Jon. 1:4). Isn't this quite interesting? God was sending a great wind to get Jonah's attention. Does this sound familiar? When we choose not to obey the voice of God, there is always a wind of opposition that comes to set us back on course. Jonah had a plan to flee from the presence of God, but God had plans to realign Jonah. I am so thankful that God will chasten them whom he loves. We all can have a tendency to do what we think is best for us, but God knows what's best for us. God doesn't choose people who cannot complete the mission. God chooses people he will help complete the mission!

While Jonah was on this boat sleeping, the mariners and ship master grew afraid and asked Jonah to call on the name of his God that none of them would perish. These men began to cast lots to determine who was responsible for this great evil coming on them. The lots fell on Jonah, and the men of that ship began to question Jonah about who he was and where he was from.

Jonah answered, "I am a Hebrew; and I fear the Lord, the God of heaven, which hath made the sea and the dry land. Then were the men exceedingly afraid, and said unto him, Why hast thou done this? For the men knew that he fled from the presence of the Lord, because he had told them. Then said they unto him, What shall we do unto thee, that the sea may be calm unto us? For the sea wrought, and was tempestuous. And he said unto them, take me up, and cast me forth into the sea; so, shall the sea be calm unto you: for I know that for my sake this great tempest is upon you" (Jon. 1:9–12).

Notice that the sea was behaving violently toward the ship as a result of Jonah's disobedience. Have you ever wanted something so bad that no matter what you were trying to do, the situation would not cooperate with you? Well, it is because you were out of the will of God. Most people think that it's warfare that's fighting them from accomplishing what they need to accomplish. Nevertheless, it could be disobedience. Warfare is a strategy of the enemy to make you miss your time, but the wind of God will bring you back where you need to be. The right prayer will dismantle warfare, but who can contend with God and win? Jonah was asking the men to throw him overboard, and when they did, there was a great calm in the sea in view of the fact that Jonah had been swallowed by a whale. Jonah prayed in the belly of this great fish, and God heard his prayer and allowed the fish to vomit him out.

Jonah was out of the fish's belly and landed in Nineveh! Are you surprised that Jonah was right where he needed to be once he agreed to do the will of God? That's a word for you! Once you agree to do the will of God, you will land right where you need to be! Don't let your disobedience cost you time outside the will of God. Some people go through years with being out of touch with God and the voice of God. Time does matter. It's everything! Jonah was in the belly of hell for three nights on account of him choosing to do what he wanted to do and not what God said. This could have been avoided if he would have heeded the voice of God. I can imagine that the belly of that fish didn't smell like a bed of roses. Have you ever felt like you landed in the wrong place in your life? Why live life with a list of regrets when you can live as an overcomer. We all have felt as if we didn't want to tackle the task that has been set before us due to some issue that we had with ourselves or maybe even others; however, we must keep our commitment to God and ask him for strength in the journey. Don't have a setback when, in fact, God is trying to set you up for the best years to come!

Brokenness

Have you ever wondered why brokenness is necessary in the life of believers? I want to draw your attention to Jeremiah 18:2–6: "Arise, and go down to the potter's house, and there I will cause thee to hear my words. Then I went down to the potter's house, and, behold, he wrought a work on the wheels. And the vessel that he made of clay was marred in the hand of the potter; so he made it again another vessel, as seemed good to the potter to make it. Then the word of the Lord came to me, saying, O house of Israel, cannot I do with you as this potter? Saith the Lord. Behold, as the clay is in the potter's hand, so are ye in mine hand, O house of Israel." Rejoice, dearly beloved. You are in the hand of your God the potter! God is going to cause you to hear the Word of the Lord, but you will be placed in a strategic posture. Where is God causing the word of revelation to come to Jeremiah? Is it not at the potter's house? God will allow brokenness to place you in the right location in order for you to hear the Word of the Lord. God is going to speak to you in the midst of your broken pieces.

Now, look at verse 3 in the above paragraph. God himself was making something on the wheel. You thought you were only going in circles on account of being lost, but you were going in circles by reason of God giving you a new beginning! Sometimes God will allow pressure to surround you in view of him shaping you to become the best version of yourself. It is, in fact, your brokenness that places you on the wheel to be molded into his perfection for your life. If God doesn't allow you to be broken, how will you hear? Most people think if it's not broken, then don't fix it. Isaiah 55:8 says, "For my thoughts are not your thoughts, neither are your ways my ways, saith the Lord." It is important that we understand the mind of God for our lives.

What you may judge as being perfect God sees as imperfect. A functioning alcoholic thinks that everything is fine given they are able to maintain a somewhat stable life. However, things are not fine. They are on the verge of losing valuable relationships due to them being consumed by their addiction. It's the same way with God. There can be things in you that will destroy you later in life if God doesn't help you rid yourself of issues of the heart, mind, and soul.

You must also understand that you can never empathize with people if you have never been broken before. When your perception of yourself is clouded by arrogance, pride, and self-righteousness, you feel you don't need anything, until you know what it is to squirm in discomfort and uncertainty. God is indeed a mastermind behind His handiwork. There are various stories in the Bible where the people of God got off track and God allowed them to be captured, persecuted, mistreated, desolate, and broken. This was God's way of indicating to His people that they will always need Him, and there is a consequence when you choose to serve other gods rather than your God. Your idols will always anger and provoke God to jealousy. Remember the Scripture is clear when it states that God is a jealous God, and put no other gods before him (Exod. 20:3–5). Often times, people idolize their occupations. They will spend countless hours researching, working overtime, and volunteering to achieve a promotion, but where is their tenacity for seeking God? When your testimony is, "I rely on God for all things," that's simply because God gave you a lesson before he released the blessing! There is nothing wrong with having confidence in your employer or things that always yield a consistent result, but your faith must arrive to a place that if anything changes, God is always your source and answer.

Being broken is not an adventure of riding a roller coaster or riding in a race car. It is an event where you are forced to look within yourself and come to a conclusion that you need God and you need him now or you will not survive! When real brokenness is in effect, you need a solution. You stop pointing the finger and start facing the problem. Hurt is different from brokenness, although sometimes, they both work together when you are facing real-life crises. When you are hurt, you don't yet recognize that you are seeing things out of the scope of your pain. But when you are broken, you realize that God has to fix this! We all would like to believe that we are well put together and have no underlining issues that will cause us to deviate from the will of God, but the truth of the matter is we all have weaknesses that we must submit to God in order to stay in perfect alignment with his will for our lives. The moment we recognize that it is impossible to be whole without the help of God is the moment where we can be put back together again!

What are weaknesses? The dictionary defines it as the state or condition of lacking strength or a person or thing that one is unable to resist or likes excessively. So how does weakness and brokenness tie in together? Your weakness may be the cause of your brokenness. Let's consider a person who is married, but infidelity is always a part of their marriage. The weakness is their inability to say no and their lack of self-control to honor their commitment to their spouse. That person can feel broken because their conscious is eating away at them, and they realize, "I am going to lose the love of my life if I don't rectify this problem in my life." Brokenness will break your will in view of the fact that you have concluded that you need help, and you need it now! God will restore your soul. Hebrews 4:12 says, "For the word of God is quick, and powerful, and sharper than any two-edged sword, piercing even to the dividing asunder of soul and spirit, and of the joints and marrow, and is a discerner of the thoughts and intents of the heart." The Word of God will enter places that a psychiatrist, psychologist, and an orthopedist can never enter.

We all have weaknesses that will never be taken from us, but we can be strengthened in our weaknesses, therefore giving us the ability to choose what is right. Prayer is the solution to strengthen us in every instance. We are attracted to our weaknesses, that's why we give in to them, but brokenness will afford you the opportunity to choose right over wrong. Why? You must understand that we all have willingness or an instinct to live and not drown. Though a person could love to be near water, but if they are thrown into a river and they don't have knowledge on swimming, will they not begin to kick, flap their arms, and scream for help? They do not want to go under though they love the sound of moving water and the scenery of water. No one wants to be consumed by their weaknesses. We all want to survive and become strong! Weaknesses are there to show us our humanity that we will always need a savior to pull us out of the water, and his name is *Jesus*!

Rejection

Rejection is something that none of us volunteers to go through. In fact, we all would rather be noncontroversial than to become rejected by those we love. Let's take a look at the life of Jesus. "He came unto his own, and his own received him not" (John 1:11). Jesus himself was rejected among his own people. Quite often, he would be among his own people preaching and teaching the Holy Scriptures, and they would say, "Isn't this the carpenter's son?" because they were in unbelief about who He said He really was. Not only can you experience rejection by those you love but also those who are on the outside. Rejection can be poisonous when you allow the negativity to penetrate your spirit. It will stimulate mixed emotions that can handicap you for the rest of your life if not properly dealt with. One of those emotions is called bitterness. I have seen bitterness break up entire families that never reconcile their differences. I will not suggest to you that this is an easy process, but I present to you that it is a work in progress because you have to be able to forgive men their trespasses.

How does one overcome rejection? It takes the Word of God graphed in your heart and the help of the Holy Spirit. The spirit of rejection will lead you to believe that you are inadequate and cause you to go into hiding. The Word has to lodge in your total being in order to work. For instance, it's not enough to be a hearer only of the Word but a doer as well. When the Word finds a place in you, the Word itself will speak up for you! That's why the Bible says the word of the Lord is "nigh thee, even in thy mouth" (Rom. 10:8). The Word is a living Word, but it needs your breath to utter outside of your mouth. So, when you breathe on the Word, you release God, because no one can speak for long periods of time without breathing. Let the Word of God dwell in you and live in you! Your freedom depends on it. The Word is the remedy for rejection! There are various knowledge in the world, but only the Word is a permanent fix for all things. "Heaven and earth will pass away but my words shall not pass away" (Matt. 24:35).

Personally, in my life, I've had to deal with the spirit of rejection more than once. I have dealt with it in ministry as well as in my childhood.

As I recall mentioning being molested by different men, one of those men said to me, "I no longer need you anymore. I have a girlfriend now." Can you imagine how that made me feel? I was only seven years old, and a teenage boy was telling me that he used me only for the pleasures of his own flesh. I was crushed on the inside. I felt as if someone was taking my life from me. I felt like I was being rejected for something better. I grew up with that for many years. Not feeling attractive enough and always hiding myself from the world. I had an image I wanted the world to see of me but not who I really was. Rejection taught me to be tough and even sometimes not sympathetic enough. I wanted to seem strong, but really, I was vulnerable, gentle, and compassionate. Later in life, I had to undress myself. I had to take off the attire of the accuser and put on the new man who is renewed in knowledge after the image of him that created him (Col. 3:10).

Rejection can either drive you into a cave or cause your actions to stem from anger and bitterness. I have spoken to many believers who were rejected, and altogether, they behaved as if being in a cave was the norm. The cave in my opinion represents depression. Many Christians refer to the prophet Elijah hiding in a cave from Jezebel as if he was waiting on God to give him his next instruction, but God himself says to the prophet, "What are you doing here?"

God does not want us hiding in caves for protection and shelter. He wants us to hide in the secret chambers of his glory. The Word of God is an active Word! If we truly have a relationship with the Word, it compels us to do what is right. It may take us some time because of our humanity, but it perfects those things that concern us. We are overcomers through the Lord Jesus Christ, and you will overcome! I understand that sometimes, when you are in the midst of the fire, it seems easier said than done; however, it is feasible. All things are possible through our Lord and savior Jesus Christ.

Don't allow the spirit of rejection to write the next chapter of your life. It is a sneaky spirit that comes to claim your future. You will live as if someone owes you something when really you owe it to yourself to be free from the opinions of others. Live your life according to the thoughts of the Father in heaven. Remember what it is that he says about you. Embrace his love for you and move forward!

About the Author

 Valerie Harris was born in Huntsville, Alabama. She grew up in the Presbyterian church but decided to explore a personal relationship with God for herself. As a result of this, she left the Presbyterian church on a mission to find her true purpose and assignment and, consequently, was called into the nondenominational church, where she met her husband, Tyler Harris.

Now married, while living a lifestyle with meaning and knowing her purpose, she received some alarming news that would forever impact her life. She was told by her gynecologist that she had endometriosis, and this could prevent her from having a family. This was a time in her life where she had to exercise her faith and petition God for a solution. Valerie witnessed and received the healing power of God. God supernaturally healed her and blessed her womb with two children.

She and her husband, Tyler Harris, are founders and pastors of Refreshed Kingdom Center Church located in Knoxville, Tennessee. She focuses on preaching the gospel, equipping lives for the purpose of the kingdom, and teaching and demonstrating healing in the life of believers.